Contents

Cosmic light shows

*Sunlight is made up of a **spectrum**, or range, of colors. When it hits Earth's **atmosphere**, sunlight is bent into rays of red, orange, yellow, green, blue, and violet.*

The sky is our window to the **cosmos**, or universe. It is filled with fascinating and spectacular sights! Some light shows such as a sunset, a full moon, or a beautiful starry night are common events. Others, like comets and auroras, are rare. Some cosmic light shows happen close to our planet, and others occur billions of miles away. Which are your favorite light shows?

Rainbows are earthly light shows caused by a cosmic body—the Sun. As sunlight passes through raindrops, it splits into six colors. The result is an arc of colored light. The complete rainbow is actually a circle, but not all of it can be seen from ground level.

(above) A sunset and full moon are two familiar light shows in the sky. In this picture, we can see both at once.

(right) Everyone loves a beautiful sunset! The sky in this picture is red because the red part of light is able to travel farther than the other colors. (See diagram on page 4.)

The Sun

The Sun is a star. It is the closest star to Earth. Without energy from the Sun, nothing could survive on Earth. There would be no color, either. All the colors that we see on Earth come from the colors in sunlight.

Ouch, that's hot!

The Sun is Earth's giant fireplace. To produce energy, it burns millions of tons of fuel each second. It has been burning for 5 billion years and is expected to burn for another 5 billion.

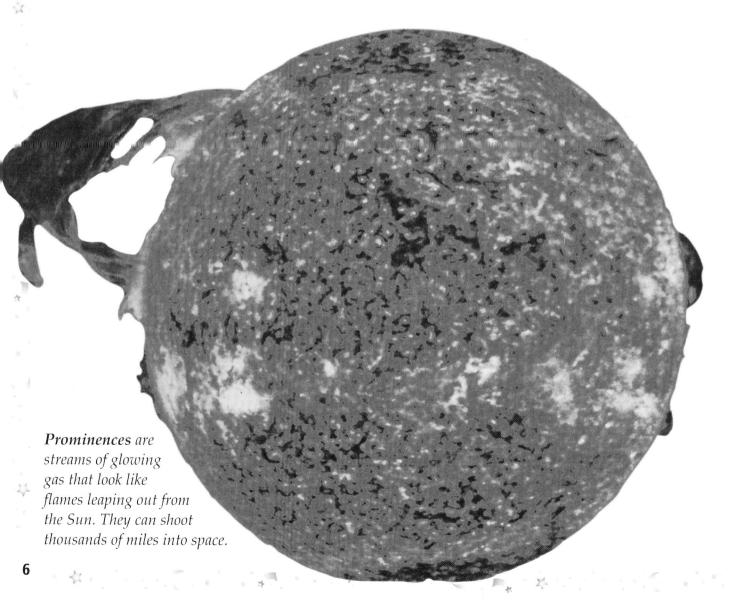

Prominences are streams of glowing gas that look like flames leaping out from the Sun. They can shoot thousands of miles into space.

The solar system

The solar system includes the Sun, nine planets, their moons, and dust, rocks, and ice. Everything **orbits**, or travels around, the Sun. Some objects have a long, oval orbit. They travel far into space. Some have shorter orbits.

Inner and outer planets

The four planets closest to the Sun are Mercury, Venus, Earth, and Mars. These planets are made up mainly of rock. They are called the **inner planets** and are part of the **inner solar system**.

Jupiter, Saturn, Uranus, and Neptune are the **outer planets**. These four planets are made up mainly of gases. The outer planets, their moons, and any other material in space are all part of the **outer solar system**. The ninth planet, Pluto, does not belong to either group. It is believed to be made of rock like the inner planets, but it is far from the Sun.

*Asteroids are huge pieces of rock that orbit the Sun between Mars and Jupiter. This ring of asteroids is called the **asteroid belt**. Asteroids range in size from a few miles wide to the size of a large city.*

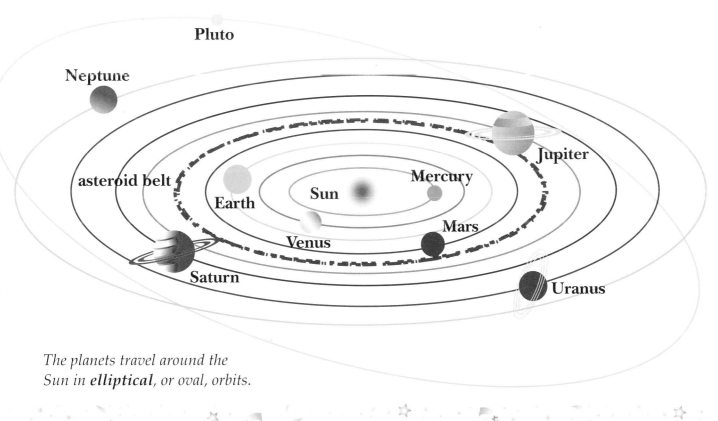

*The planets travel around the Sun in **elliptical**, or oval, orbits.*

What is a star?

Inside a star there are millions of explosions every second. They give off energy and make the star glow.

Stars are balls of burning gases. Many stars are like the Sun but are much farther away. Some are thousands of times larger than the Sun, but most are about one-quarter the size. Small stars cannot be seen without a telescope.

Why does a star shine?

Imagine you had a tiny balloon in your hand. If you squeezed your hand tighter and tighter around the balloon, the balloon would pop. A similar thing happens to stars. Each star has hydrogen and other gases at its center. **Gravity** causes the star to squeeze tightly together. The gases in the center heat up. As the gases get hotter, the hydrogen burns, causing explosions.

What a lovely couple

Everything in the universe is orbiting something else. Stars are moving, too. Many stars that you see in the sky are actually two stars. Most stars travel close together in pairs. They are attracted to each other by the pull of their gravity. Pairs of stars are called **double stars**. Most pairs are twins. They are the same age and were born in the same place, at the same time. Sometimes double stars shoot gas at each other, making a colorful streamer in the sky.

A star is born

A nebula looks thick and dense like a cotton ball, but it is actually misty like steam from a kettle. It looks thick because the particles of dust and gas are lit by the stars around it.

Nebulae are clouds of dust and gas. Some people call them "stellar nurseries" because stars are created there. Gravity causes particles of dust and gas in the nebula to stick together. The particles form **globules**, or spheres. When the globules begin to glow, they become stars.

Burning hot!

Stars appear white in the night sky, but they are actually different colors. Their color depends on how big and how hot they are.

When metal is heated, it becomes red-hot. With more heat, it turns orange, yellow, and then white-hot. The same is true of stars.

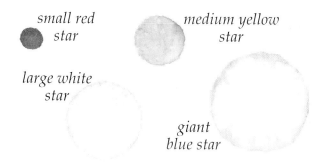

small red star

medium yellow star

large white star

giant blue star

Giant blue stars burn more hydrogen than any other stars. They are the largest stars.

Different colors

Small stars are red. They are not as hot as other stars. Red stars can shine up to 40 billion years because they burn hydrogen slowly. Medium-sized stars, like our Sun, are yellow. Large stars glow white-hot. They burn more hydrogen than smaller stars.

Death of a star

When a star has burned up most of its gases in the center, it swells up like a giant beach ball and then collapses and shrinks into a tiny star. With the last of its energy, the tiny star glows white and is called a **white dwarf**. After the white dwarf cools off, a chunk of black rock, called a **black dwarf**, remains.

Novas and supernovas

Often one star in a pair sends too much gas to its partner, causing the second star to overheat and explode. This event is called a **nova explosion**, and the star is called a **nova**. Part of the star is blown away in the explosion, but it is not completely destroyed. When a star explodes, the particles of dust and gas that made up the star become part of the nebula again.

Blown apart

Sometimes very large stars explode completely. A star can become so large that gravity forces it to collapse. In less than a second, the star blows apart. The huge explosion that occurs is called a **supernova**. Supernovas glow millions of times brighter than the Sun! There have been only three supernovas in the Milky Way.

In a nova explosion, one star in a pair receives too much gas from its partner. It flares brightly and loses some of its dust and gas. The star then returns to its original color.

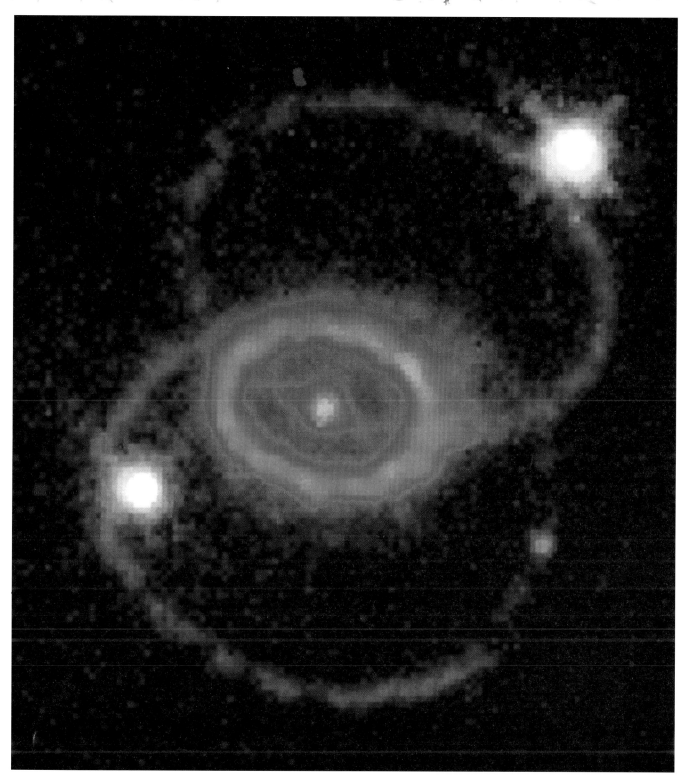

This picture shows a star being destroyed in a supernova explosion.

Constellations

A constellation is a group of stars that appears to form a picture. There are 88 different constellations. Some look like animals, some look like objects, and a few even resemble people. The Big Dipper looks like a ladle, or dipper, that is used to serve soup from a pot. People who live north of the **equator** see different constellations than those who live south of the equator.

Constellations that appear in summer are different from those that can be seen in winter. As Earth orbits the Sun, we get a different view of space. The four constellations shown on these pages can be seen from the northern hemisphere at the times listed under the pictures. The dots represent stars. The size of the dot tells us how bright the star is. The larger the dot, the brighter the star.

Orion can be seen from December to March.

Taurus is best seen from October to March.

1. In Greek myths, Orion was a mighty hunter who was killed by a scorpion. The Orion constellation has some of the brightest stars in our solar system. Betelgeuse, the star on Orion's left shoulder, and Rigel, located on the right leg, are **supergiants**.

2. Taurus the bull has two large star **clusters**, or groups. The first cluster, Pleiades, is located in the bull's shoulder. The second cluster, Hyades, outlines the bull's snout.

3. The two brightest stars in Gemini are named after the twin sons of the Roman god Jupiter. Pollux, in the left twin's head, is a very bright yellow-orange star. Castor, in the right twin's head, is actually a multiple star made of three double stars.

4. The Big and Little Dippers look like two ladles in the sky. Polaris, which is located at the end of the Little Dipper's handle, is the most famous star in our sky. It is also called the North Star.

Gemini is best seen from December to May.

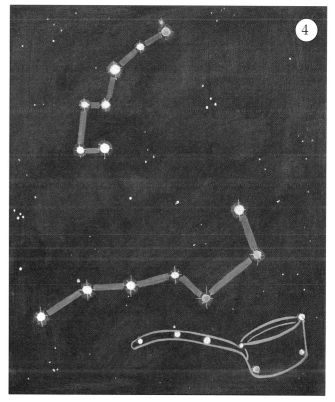

The Big and Little Dippers can be seen year round.

Galaxies

Stars are not scattered evenly throughout the universe. They are grouped together in huge star systems called **galaxies**. Scientists believe that there are billions of galaxies in our universe. From Earth, stars in a galaxy appear to be on top of one another, but stars are usually many **light-years** apart. The stars in a galaxy are held together by gravity.

Space begins about 100 miles (160 km) above the ground, where the Earth's atmosphere ends.

Getting bigger

The universe is always expanding, as galaxies move farther away from one another. Despite the great size and large number of galaxies, the universe is mostly open space.

Spilled milk?

Our solar system is part of a large group of stars and planets called the **Milky Way** galaxy. The Milky Way is so large that light coming from a star on one side of the galaxy would take 100,000 years to reach the other side.

Our galaxy is named the Milky Way because it looks like a puddle of spilled milk in the sky.

Types of galaxies

There are three main types of galaxies—**spiral**, **elliptical**, and **irregular**. Some astronomers claim that **barred spirals** are a fourth type of galaxy.

The Milky Way is an example of a spiral galaxy. It a looks like a pinwheel with arms spinning around a central bulge. The oldest stars are in the central bulge, and the younger stars are in the bright, starry arms. From the side, spiral galaxies look like fried eggs.

Elliptical galaxies do not have arms. They can range in shape from **spherical**, or round, to a long, flat, cigar shape. Some elliptical galaxies are small. Large elliptical galaxies, the largest galaxies in the universe, may be the result of a few galaxies joining together.

Spiral galaxies have starry arms that spiral out from the center.

Most elliptical galaxies are oval-shaped. Some have ten times the number of stars as a spiral galaxy.

Barred spirals have starry arms that come from a bar in the center, rather than from the bulge itself.

Irregular galaxies do not have a particular shape. This galaxy is called the Large Magellanic Cloud.

Comets

Comets are balls of frozen gas and dust that orbit the outer solar system. Astronomers believe that some comets come from the **Oort Cloud**, which is thought to be a sphere of comets that surrounds the solar system.

Sometimes the gravity of a planet or a passing star causes a comet to change its orbit. Comets can become part of the inner solar system when their orbit changes.

Just keep on orbiting!

Every year more than 200 comets orbit the inner solar system. Some comets have short orbits, whereas others take longer to make the trip around the Sun. Each time a comet comes close to the Sun, it loses gas and dust and its body becomes smaller. After millions of years, the comet disappears. Comets travel very slowly. It can take weeks or months for a comet to disappear from the sky.

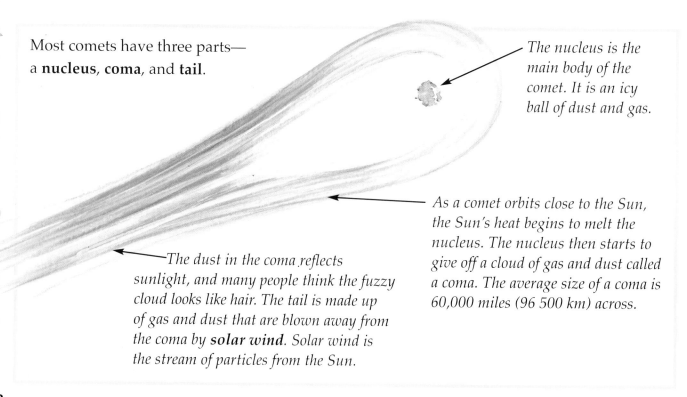

Most comets have three parts— a **nucleus**, **coma**, and **tail**.

The nucleus is the main body of the comet. It is an icy ball of dust and gas.

*The dust in the coma reflects sunlight, and many people think the fuzzy cloud looks like hair. The tail is made up of gas and dust that are blown away from the coma by **solar wind**. Solar wind is the stream of particles from the Sun.*

As a comet orbits close to the Sun, the Sun's heat begins to melt the nucleus. The nucleus then starts to give off a cloud of gas and dust called a coma. The average size of a coma is 60,000 miles (96 500 km) across.

Famous comets

Halley's comet, shown above, was named after Edmond Halley. In 1705, Halley guessed that comets had regular orbits. He predicted that a comet that appeared above London in 1682 would return 76 years later. He was right! Since then, people have been studying comets more closely. Halley's comet is scheduled to return in the year 2061. Many countries have sent probes into space to study the comet.

Comet Hale-Bopp (shown right) was discovered in 1995, over a year and a half before it entered the inner solar-system orbit in 1997. Hale-Bopp will not be seen from Earth again until the year 5995!

Asteroids and meteors

Chunks of rock and metal orbit the Sun. This **debris** is believed to be left over from the creation of planets, stars, and moons.

Asteroids are the largest space rocks. They come from the asteroid belt, a ring of asteroids between Mars and Jupiter. (See page 7.)

asteroid

Sometimes they are pulled out of their orbit by the gravity of a passing planet, which hurls them through space.

Meteoroids are pieces of asteroids or comets. Most meteoroids burn up when they hit Earth's atmosphere. Large meteoroids that survive the trip through the atmosphere and land on the ground are called **meteorites**.

Some scientists believe that a giant meteorite caused the dinosaurs to become extinct. When the meteorite hit the ground, a cloud of dust rose up and blocked out the Sun. Most plants and animals died because of the lack of sunlight. When the dust settled, the dinosaurs were dead.

Crashing to Earth

The Moon and planets close to the asteroid belt, such as Jupiter, Mars, and Earth, have many **craters**, or bowl-shaped holes. The craters were formed long ago when asteroids crashed into these bodies. Some of Earth's craters are now lakes, but most of them have been **eroded**, or smoothed out, over time. When Earth formed an atmosphere, fewer **impacts**, or hits, occurred.

Shooting stars

Have you ever seen a bright streak of light travel through the night sky and then quickly disappear? You may have seen a **meteor**. When a meteoroid burns up inside Earth's atmosphere, hot, melted material streams off behind it. The burning meteoroid and its tail are called a meteor. As it burns, its dust falls to Earth. Twenty-five tons of meteor dust fall to Earth each day!

*Sometimes Earth experiences a cosmic fireworks display known as a **meteor shower**. This event happens when Earth passes through a comet's tail or a large group of meteors. When these particles enter Earth's atmosphere, they burn up and look like bright ashes falling through the sky.*

The Moon

The Moon has no atmosphere to scatter the Sun's rays. Sunsets and blue skies do not exist there—the Moon's sky is always black. Still, the Moon does put on its own show! It is nature's biggest movie screen. Sunlight is projected onto the Moon's surface and is then reflected back to Earth. The Moon is made mostly of rock and minerals and its rough, cratered surface can be seen from Earth.

Where did it go?

Just as Earth orbits the Sun, the Moon orbits Earth. Earth, the Moon, and the Sun are always changing positions. As the Moon moves through its orbit, we see different amounts of the Moon's lit surface. To us, the Moon appears to change shape. Sometimes the entire Moon reflects sunlight. Sometimes only half or a quarter appears to have sunlight on it. We see these shapes in the sky.

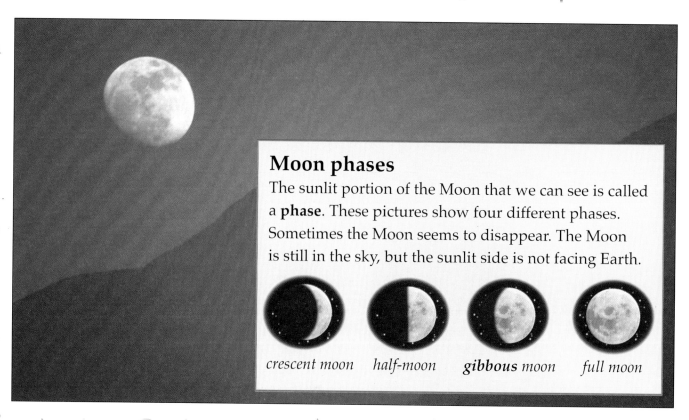

Moon phases

The sunlit portion of the Moon that we can see is called a **phase**. These pictures show four different phases. Sometimes the Moon seems to disappear. The Moon is still in the sky, but the sunlit side is not facing Earth.

crescent moon   *half-moon*   ***gibbous** moon*   *full moon*

You see the Moon in the sky mostly at night, but if you lived on the Moon, you would get a different view. You would see Earth all the time because the sky is always dark on the Moon!

Other moons

Earth's Moon is called "the Moon," but in fact, there are over 60 moons orbiting the other eight planets in our solar system. Jupiter has 16 moons, and Saturn has 18 moons! All these moons reflect the Sun's light, just as our Moon does. They do not appear as bright as Earth's Moon, however, because they are farther away from Earth. This picture shows a few of Saturn's many moons.

Lunar eclipses

The Moon does not make its own light. It only appears to be lit up because it reflects sunlight. Sometimes, as Earth and the Moon follow their orbits, they line up with the Sun in a straight line. If Earth is lined up between the Sun and the Moon, it blocks the Sun and casts a shadow on the Moon. We call this event a **lunar eclipse**. There are one or two lunar eclipses each year.

Earth's shadow has two parts—the **umbra** and **penumbra**. The umbra is the dark, central part of the shadow. The gray outer part of the shadow is called the penumbra. When the Moon moves into Earth's penumbra, it is dimmed but not blocked out. A total eclipse occurs when the Moon moves into Earth's dark umbra. When only part of the umbra falls on the Moon, it is called a partial lunar eclipse.

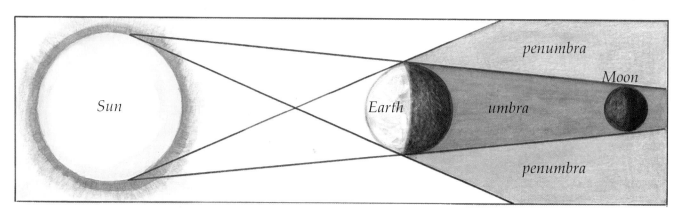

Red light

During a total lunar eclipse, the Moon is not completely dark. It glows a dark orangy-red color. The Moon itself does not change color, however. During a lunar eclipse, some of the Sun's rays pass through Earth's atmosphere. The atmosphere bends the sunlight and separates it into different colors. (See diagram on page 4.) The long red and orange rays pass through the atmosphere and reflect off the Moon's surface, causing it to glow orangy-red.

This special photograph shows the Moon as it moves across the sky during a lunar eclipse. An eclipse can be seen from anywhere on Earth where it is nighttime.

Solar eclipses

Once in a while, the Sun gets dark in the middle of the day. Thousands of years ago, people believed that a great dragon swept down from the sky and gobbled up the Sun. They beat drums, trying to frighten the dragon away. Today, we know that when the Sun disappears, we are seeing a **solar eclipse**.

How an eclipse happens

Earth orbits the Sun once a year. At the same time, the Moon orbits Earth. An eclipse occurs when the Sun, the Moon, and Earth are lined up.

Solar eclipses happen when the Moon passes between the Sun and Earth. The Moon's shadow falls on part of Earth, blocking our view of the Sun.

Where did the Sun go?

The Sun is much larger than the Moon, but it is farther from Earth. The Moon has an elliptical orbit. During part of its orbit, the Moon is closer to Earth than it is at other times.

A total eclipse occurs when the Moon's orbit brings it closer to Earth, making it appear to be the same size as the Sun, which is much farther away. When the Moon moves in front of the Sun, it blocks the Sun out from our view. The Moon orbits Earth in a tilted path, so the Moon does not always line up perfectly between the Sun and Earth. A total eclipse happens once or twice a year. From any one location on Earth, it is visible only once every 360 years.

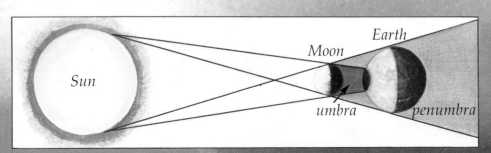

Sun · Moon · Earth · umbra · penumbra

This background picture shows an annular eclipse. The edge of the Sun is still visible.

Full eclipse

The Moon has many hills and valleys caused by meteors and asteroids that have crashed into it. The bumpy surface of the Moon scatters the Sun's rays. During a total eclipse, rays from the **corona**, the Sun's outer layer, become visible and shine a soft, pearly light far beyond the Moon.

Baily's beads

Circles of glowing light appear around the darkened Sun during a total eclipse. They are called Baily's beads because they were discovered in 836 by Francis Baily. Sometimes the beads look like a diamond ring in the sky.

Partial eclipse

A partial eclipse happens when Earth, the Moon, and the Sun do not line up perfectly. Only part of the Sun is blocked out. The Sun looks like a cookie with a bite taken out of it.

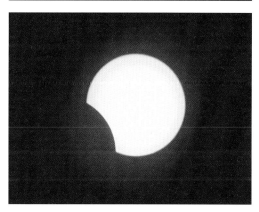

Annular eclipse

When the Moon is in the distant part of its orbit, it appears to be smaller than the Sun. When the Moon moves in front of the Sun, it cannot completely block out the Sun. In an annular eclipse, we are still able to see a ring of the Sun around the Moon.

Do not look!
Harmful rays called radiation become stronger during a total solar eclipse and can cause blindness. Never look directly at a solar eclipse, even through a camera or binoculars!

Auroras

Auroras are curtains of light that hang in the sky. They can be seen only from certain places on Earth. Auroras above the North Pole are called **aurora borealis**, or northern lights. Those around the South Pole are called **aurora australis**, or southern lights.

Storms on the Sun

Auroral lights are caused by storms on the Sun. The heat of the Sun causes particles in its outer layer to break apart. These particles are called **plasma**.

As the Sun rotates, plasma is flung off into space as **solar wind**. Earth has a magnetic field, which attracts plasma to the North and South Poles.

Attracting plasma

Huge explosions cause **solar flares**, which send extra plasma into space. The plasma is trapped by Earth's magnetic field. Plasma spirals toward Earth and collides with particles in the atmosphere, causing them to glow. This glow is called an aurora.

Aurora facts

Auroral lights are mainly green, blue, and red. The lights may appear as an arc, dancing rays, or a shimmering curtain.

People who live near the North and South poles see the same auroral lights at the same time. They can see the lights 243 times per year. Some auroras can stretch 1,000 miles (1600 km) across the sky.

Auroras can cause big problems on Earth. They scramble satellite messages, cause problems with telephone systems, and interfere with radio and television waves.

In this illustration, the red, yellow, and green lines coming from the Sun represent solar wind. The blue lines connecting Earth's poles show the magnetic field.

If I had my own spaceship...

On clear nights, I look up at the Milky Way and wish I had my very own spaceship. Think of the vacation I could take!

First, I would fly up to the Hubble Space Telescope to pick out all the best places in the universe to visit.

Then, for a warm-up, I would do flips and twirls in zero gravity in my Manned Maneuvering Unit!

Next, I'm off to the Moon to check out some moon rocks and huge craters!

On Mars, I would climb the red mountains to watch a Martian sunset. After Mars, I would investigate the fiercest storm in the solar system, Jupiter's Great Red Spot. This storm has been brewing for over 300 years!

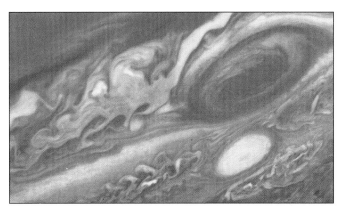

No trip to the universe would be complete without a visit to Saturn. Look at those colorful rings! A spin in the Whirlpool Galaxy sounds like fun.

Time for a *siesta* in the Sombrero Galaxy. With so many stars, planets, moons, and giant galaxies still to explore, I need to have a rest!

Write your own space adventure and draw pictures of the cosmic light shows you might see. Blastoff!

Glossary

atmosphere The gases that surround Earth

Baily's beads Bright circles of light that appear around the Moon before it covers the Sun completely during an eclipse

constellation A group of stars that appears to form a picture

eclipse The darkening of the Sun or Moon when light coming from the Sun is blocked

gibbous A phase of the Moon when more than its half is illuminated

Large Magellanic Cloud An irregular galaxy near the Milky Way that can be seen with the naked eye

light-year The distance light travels in one Earth year

Milky Way The spiral galaxy in which our solar system is found

nebula A large cloud of dust and gas from which stars are created

penumbra The outer part of the Moon's or Earth's shadow cast during an eclipse

plasma Particles on the outer layers of the Sun

solar flares Explosions on the Sun's surface that send plasma into space

solar system The Sun, all the planets, moons, and other heavenly bodies that orbit the Sun

supergiant A large star that is thousands of times larger than our Sun

umbra The dark, central part of the Moon's or Earth's shadow cast during an eclipse

Index

1 2 3 4 5 6 7 8 9 0 Printed in the U.S.A. 7 6 5 4 3 2 1 0 9 8